SCHIRMER'S LIBRARY
OF MUSICAL CLASSICS

CARL CZERNY

Op. 823

The Little Pianist

Easy Progressive Exercises

Beginning with the First Rudiments

Translated from the German by

DR. THEODORE BAKER

→ Book I — Library Vol. 55

Book II — Library Vol. 56

Complete — Library Vol. 54

ISBN 978-0-7935-5241-2

G. SCHIRMER, Inc.

DISTRIBUTED BY

HAL•LEONARD®
CORPORATION
7777 W. BLUEMOUND RD. P.O. BOX 13819 MILWAUKEE, WI 53213

Table of Notes

With an Explanation of Clefs and Staves

Bass Notes   Treble Notes

C may be written C,
c̄ may be written c',
c̿ may be written c'', etc.
C D E F G A B C D E F G A B c d e f g a b c d e f g a b c d e f g a b c d e f g a b c d e f g a
Violin-clef (also called G-clef or treble clef)
Bass clef (also called F-clef)
8va bassa
These bass notes are of just the same pitch as the notes above them in the treble clef.
Contra-Octave
Great Octave
Small Octave
One-lined Octave
Two-lined Octave
Three-lined Octave
Four-lined Octave

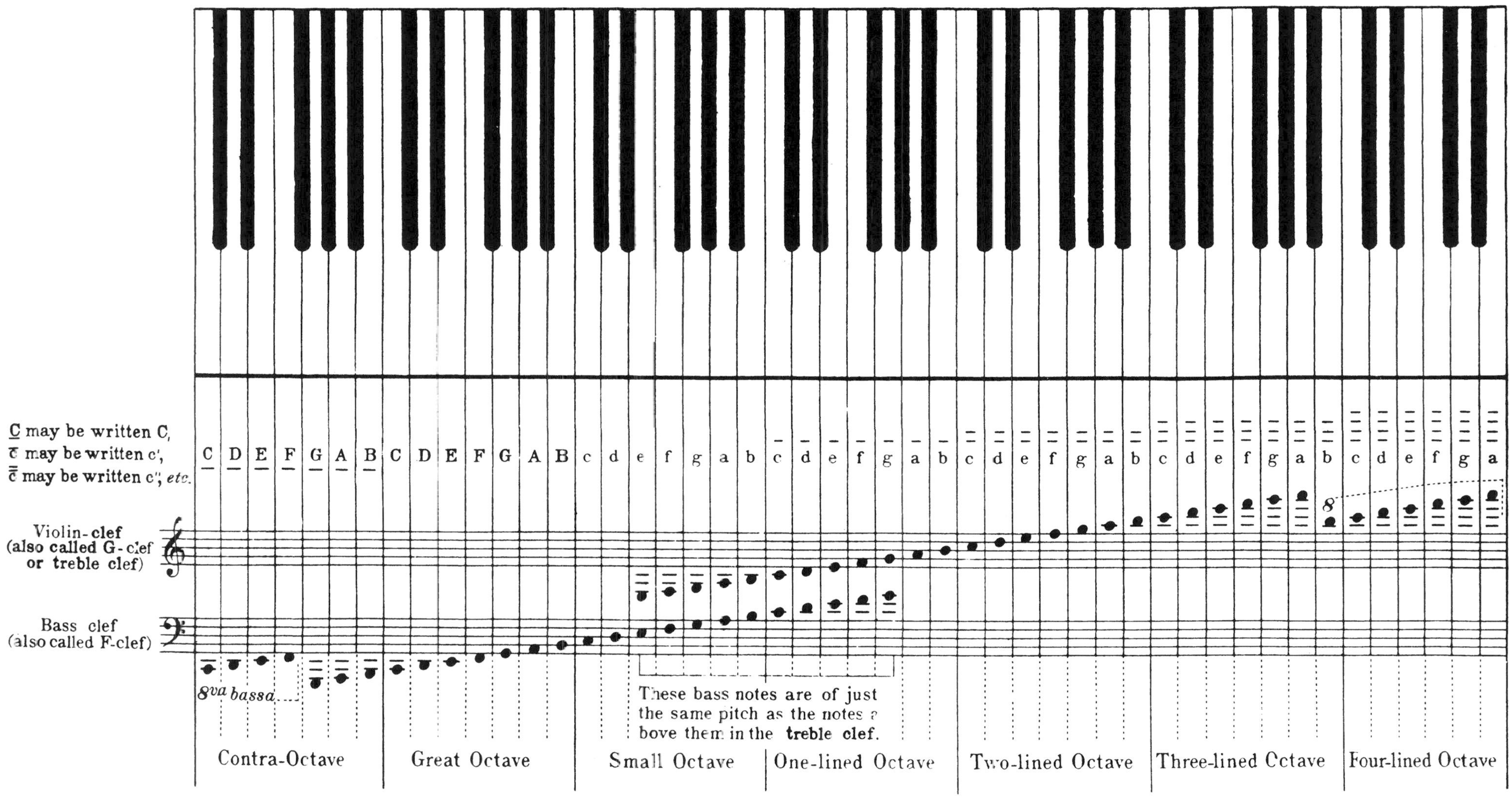

The round, black dots are called *notes*. They may be written either on the lines or in the spaces between the lines.

As shown above, each clef is set on a group of five lines. These five lines are called the *staff*. Examine the clefs carefully, and notice what effect they have on the signification of the notes.

The Rudiments of Music

The signs used to show the position (pitch, either high or low) of the tones are called *notes*. They are written on what is called the *staff*, which consists of five parallel *lines* and the *spaces* between the lines:

The lowest line (or space) is called the *first line* (or space); the next line (or space) above, the *second;* etc.: that is, both lines and spaces are counted from below upwards.

Notes that are either too high or too low to be written on the staff must be set on or between short added lines above or below. These lines are called *leger-lines.*

For naming the notes, the first seven letters of the alphabet are used. In the *key of C major* the letters come in the following order: C, D, E, F, G, A, B, ending on C. These eight notes form what is called the *scale of C major.* Every scale is composed of five whole-steps and two half-steps, which occur in the following order:

Scale of C major

A *sharp* (♯) written before a note raises it a half-step; a *flat* (♭) written before a note lowers it a half-step. A *natural* (♮) restores a note to the original pitch.

There are two *modes*, the *major* and the *minor* mode. The principal scales in the minor mode are the *melodic* and the *harmonic*.

One important difference between major and minor scales is that in the major there are four half-steps between tonic and mediant, but in the minor there are only three.

There are twelve *major keys*, the tonics or keynotes of which **are** determined by the signature. The following are the *tonic chords* of all these keys.

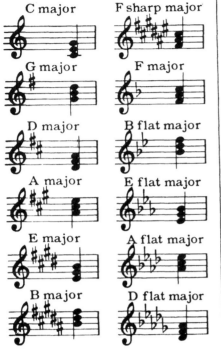

C major | F sharp major
G major | F major
D major | B flat major
A major | E flat major
E major | A flat major
B major | D flat major

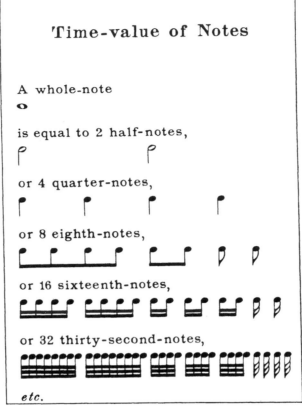

Time-value of Notes

A whole-note

is equal to 2 half-notes,

or 4 quarter-notes,

or 8 eighth-notes,

or 16 sixteenth-notes,

or 32 thirty-second-notes,

etc.

There are twelve *minor keys*, the tonics or keynotes of which are determined by the signature. The following are the *tonic chords* of all these keys.

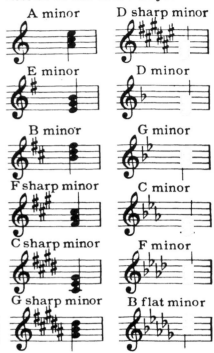

A minor | D sharp minor
E minor | D minor
B minor | G minor
F sharp minor | C minor
C sharp minor | F minor
G sharp minor | B flat minor

In writing signatures, sharps are added by skipping upwards a fifth,* then downwards a fourth,* and so on.

F sharp C sharp G sharp D sharp A sharp E sharp B sharp

* For the meaning of these intervals, see page VIII.

In writing signatures, flats are added by skipping upwards a fourth, then downwards a fifth, and so on.

B flat E flat A flat D flat G flat C flat F flat

If a note already sharp is to be raised another half-step, this sign (×), called a *double-sharp*, is used; if a note with a flat is to be lowered another half-step, the (♭♭) *double-flat* is used.

F sharp F double-sharp F sharp E flat E double-flat E flat

*The use of the ♮ in this connection is being generally discontinued.

Keys having similar signatures stand in closest relation to each other, and are called *relative keys.*

The *clefs* chiefly used are the following:

Treble or G-clef   Bass or F-clef   Soprano or C-clef   Alto Clef   Tenor Clef

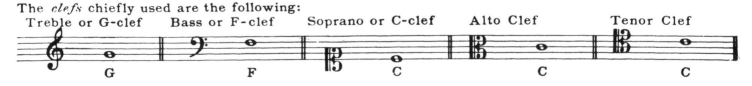

G   F   C   C   C

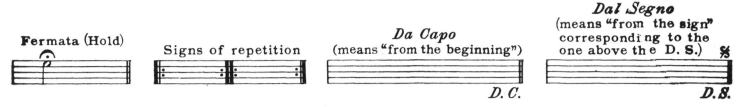

Fermata (Hold)	Signs of repetition	*Da Capo* (means "from the beginning")	*Dal Segno* (means "from the sign" corresponding to the one above the D. S.)
		D. C.	D. S.

Time-value of Rests

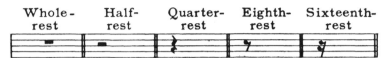

Whole- rest	Half- rest	Quarter- rest	Eighth- rest	Sixteenth- rest

When a rest occupies the time of more than one measure, the number of measures rested may be indicated by an equal number of whole rests run together, usually with a number over it, or by a heavy single or double stroke with a number over it, thus:

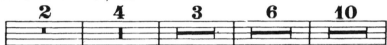

A dot set after a note or rest adds one-half to the time-value of the note or rest: | a second dot further adds half as much as the first one.

Notes									
Rests									*etc.*
Time-value:	Three halves	Three quarters	Three eighths	Three sixteenths	Seven quarters	Seven eighths	Seven sixteenths	Seven thirty-seconds	

The following abbreviations are used in notation:

written

played

A *slur* indicates that notes are to be played in a smooth and connected manner.

A *tie*, connecting two notes on the same degree, indicates that they are to be played as *one note* having the combined value of both.

If, in a regular rhythm [notation], one or more notes are played before the beats on which they are expected, thus: [notation], they are called *syncopated notes*.

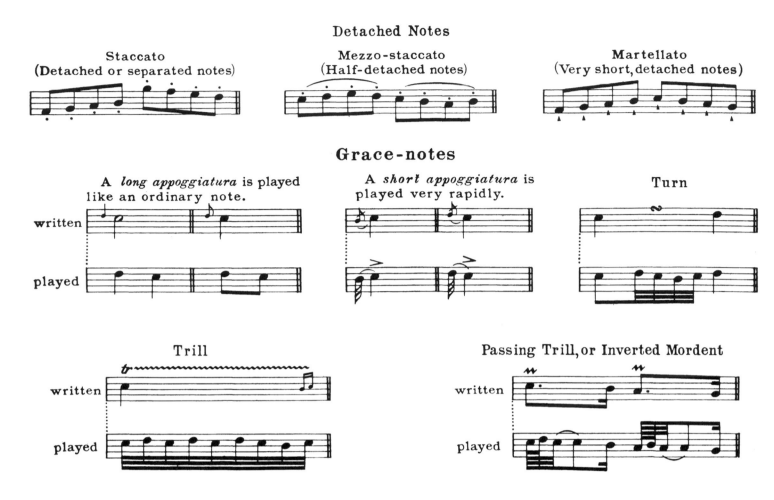

The Different Species of Time

There are two species of time: common time and triple time. These are subdivided into simple and compound Simple common time has only two beats or divisions in a measure ($\frac{2}{1}$, $\frac{2}{2}$, $\frac{2}{4}$); simple triple time contains three parts in a measure ($\frac{3}{2}$, $\frac{3}{4}$, $\frac{3}{8}$, *etc.*). When two or more simple common measures are drawn into one, it is called compound common time. Compound triple time is that in which two or more simple triple measures are drawn into one. Four quarter-notes in a measure ($\frac{4}{4}$) are indicated by **C**, other divisions by $\frac{2}{4}$, $\frac{3}{4}$, *etc.*

Intervals

The distance in pitch between two tones is termed an interval. There are seven principal intervals.

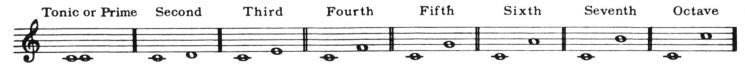

The following Italian words are used to point out the degree of slowness or quickness, or the expression of a movement: *Adagio*, slow; *Andante*, not quite so slow; *Allegro*, rapid; *Allegretto*, less rapid; *Presto*, very rapid; *p (piano)*, soft; *pp (pianissimo)*, very soft; *f (forte)*, loud; *ff (fortissimo)*, very loud and strong; *diminuendo*, gradually diminishing the tone; *crescendo*, gradually increasing the tone; *decrescendo*, decreasing the tone; *ritardando*, becoming slower, *etc.*

Whole, Half-and Quarter-notes.

CARL CZERNY. Op. 823, Book I.

Eighth-notes, Triplets and Sixteenth-notes
in Common and Triple Time.

Allegretto vivace.

35.

Exercises with ♯ ♭ and ♮

Allegro moderato.

39.

Allegretto.

40.

The Bass Notes.

The Twelve Major and Twelve Minor Scales.

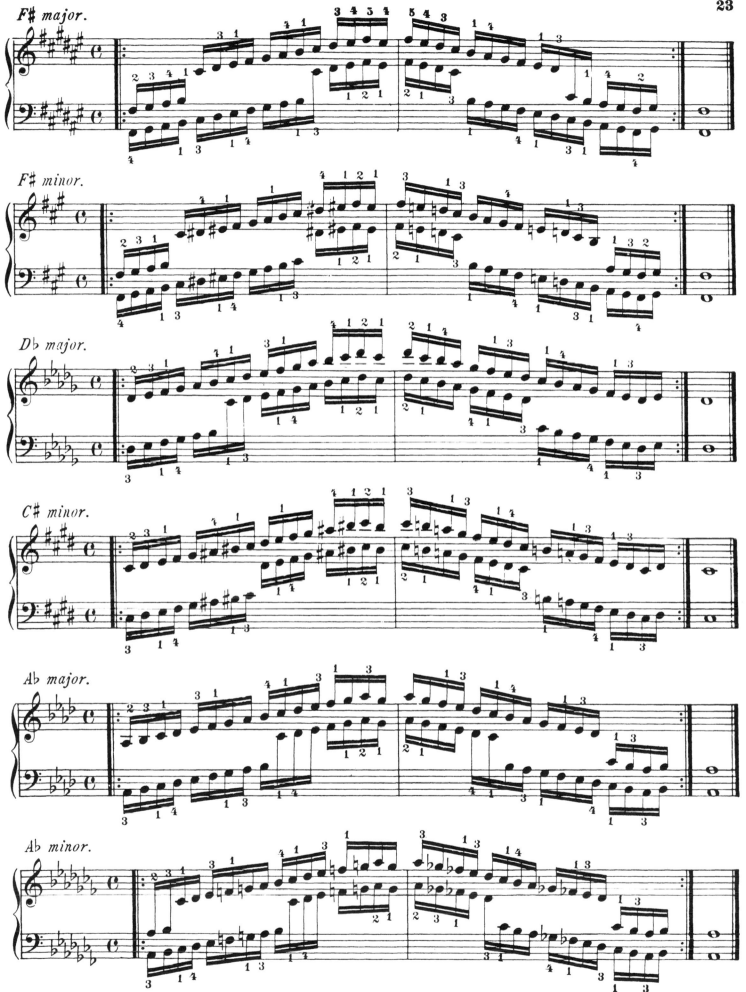

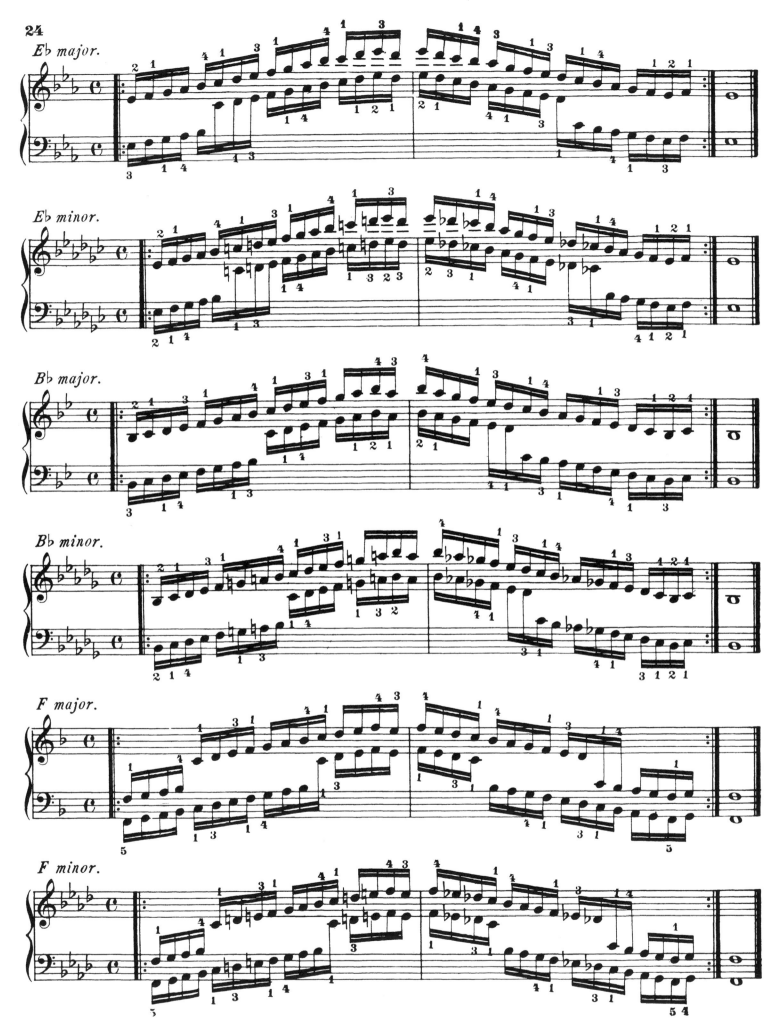